"In this spellbinding book, poet and novelist Browning spares no detail in telling the story of her descent into profound grief as one loss piled upon another. Though small, this effective and plainspoken memoir is densely packed with tales of harrowing experiences that require emotional, intellectual, and spiritual investments on the part of the reader. Browning's journey of recovery will be of help to anyone looking for courage in difficult times."

— *PUBLISHERS WEEKLY*

"A laconic, beautiful, and deeply insightful account about coping with loss."

— *KIRKUS REVIEWS*

"Browning brings us inside the disoriented unfolding of a life taking new shape after trauma. This is not a 'tie a neat bow around it' trauma and recovery story with a too-simple happy ending, but a messy, honest look at a life that will never be the same."

— *NARRATIVELY*

"Impressively candid and articulate, extraordinarily honest and insightful, exceptionally well written, organized and presented, *To Lose the Madness* is an inherently compelling read from cover to cover. Thoughtful and thought-provoking from first page to last, *To Lose the Madness* is unreservedly recommended for personal reading lists, as well as community and academic library collections."

— *MIDWEST BOOK REVIEW*

"Browning's essay explores the confluence of natural and interior landscapes in a manner both beautiful and searing."

— *FOREWORD REVIEWS*

D1564207

Drive through the night

POETIC MEMOIR ON TAMING,
RECLAIMING & BECOMING WILD

Drive through the night

POEMS & PHOTOGRAPHY BY

L.M. BROWNING

HOMEBOUND PUBLICATIONS
BERKSHIRE MOUNTAINS, MASS.

HOMEBOUND PUBLICATIONS

WWW.HOMEBOUNDPUBLICATIONS.COM

Cover Design and Interior Design by Leslie M. Browning
Cover Image: © Kevin Bosc
All Interior Images © Leslie M. Browning
with the exception of the following:
Blurred Light page 6 © Rafael Shiga | Buffalo page 28 © Lauren Mancke
Pills image on page 34 © Teslariu Mihai
Hawk Design page 109 © Justin Rakowski, Homestead Tattoos, Philadelphia PA
Photos on pages 118, 123, and 124 © Sara Mussen of AwarenessImages.com

First Edition Trade Paperback 978-1-953340450
First Edition Hardcover (Wayfarer Books, 2022) 978-1-956368-10-9
Also Available in eBook, Hardcover and Audiobook

10 9 8 7 6 5 4 3 2 1

Homebound Publications is committed to ecological stewardship. We greatly value the natural environment and invest in environmental conservation. For each book purchased in our online store we plant one tree.

DEDICATION

For all the outliers.
I see you.
You are not alone.

CONTENTS

PART 2: THE BREAKING

PART 3: THE BOLTING

PART 4: THE RECLAIMING

FINDING TRUE NORTH

WHEN I WAS YOUNGER. I kept telling myself that the latest trauma would be the last. As though life's baseline is peace, and things would eventually even out if I could only hang on. At some point, hanging on, decayed into denial, distractions, self-medicating, and self-harm.

Emptiness burned across my twenties like a wildfire. I drank but damned if that didn't make it rage harder—fuel to the inner-fire. I grew up around heroin addicts and violent alcoholics, and wanted nothing to do with any of it. The first time I got drunk, I was 27. The thing I loved most about being drunk was I didn't have to think *about it all*—

Long story short, the drinking was classic self-medicating. I suffered from Complex Post Traumatic Stress Syndrome and other effects from prolonged exposure to poverty and abuse. The whiskey facilitated my denial; it gave me a reprieve from the burden of memory, but the emptiness burned fiercer.

I wasn't empty because others abandoned me, but because I had abandoned myself. Who I am was repressed—collateral damage in a long-term coping mechanism gone unchecked. My subconscious had put up partitions to contain the flood of emotion in the wake of trauma, but in doing so, my identity was trapped and locked away as well. As a result, everything repressed would one day come forward—without warning, without control, and without a shutoff valve.

Survival is balance. Life's ugliness is balanced by beauty. Trauma is balanced by awe. For me, being on the road has come to represent awe-seeking—what I find in the still-wild places is counterbalance to the traumas.

The poetry in this collection is pulled from my notebooks; they were written before, during, and after I began to understand who I am. They were written across the nights—while traveling the distance between who I was expected to become and who I authentically—irrevocably—am.

I'm a spiritual mutt. The road is my church. It was on the road that I discovered the landscape god. My journals tell of the perpetual midnight mass held on the highways and byways of the American West. Every so often, climbing out of the driver's seat with a journal and a camera, seeking the sacrament of the wild silence found in the unsullied sanctuaries of intact wilderness.

This book is divided into four parts: "The Taming," "The Breaking," "The Bolting," and "The Reclaiming." These sections trace a fitful pursuit of the white-picket-fence life with all the domesticated pillars we are taught compose a successful life.

While happiness was my pursuit, the tone of these pages is one of torment, grief, addiction, distraction, emptiness, infidelity, self-harm, and despair—all manner of maladapted coping mechanisms I developed as I tried to shape myself to fit the template of this American life, which in all its toxicity, is killing us.

This poetic pseudo-memoir spans years of my life wherein I suffered a dumbfounding amount of trauma. There were so many times in my twenties and thirties that I told myself at the end of the latest blindside that the worst was behind me—that this was the end of the bad and the beginning of a better time. Telling myself that was simultaneously what kept me going and what made it all the harder when the suffering would, of course, return. But that is how coping mechanisms are; they keep us going until they start holding us back.

Silence is central to my life; it is an element I actively seek and require for balance. Consequently, a recurring theme in my work has been silence. I primarily focus on what I term "wild silence," which embodies a healthy silence found within the landscape while in the flow of awe.

The quality of silence in my life speaks to the health of my soul/mind. If the silence is deafening, suppressive, terrifying (it speaks to a fever raging silently in the psyche because the life I am living doesn't align with your core values and/or the presence of something or someone harmful.)

This quality of silence holds within it the unfelt, the unsaid, the unspeakable, the unrecognized, the unhealed, the unreconciled, the unconscionable . . . in addressing what lives in the silence and learning how to tolerate it—sit with it—we begin the work necessary to integrate the parts of ourselves sequestered into suppression. In *Drive Through the Night*, as in my own life, the silence is present, forward, and telling.

In the last seven years, another central theme in my life has been identity. I have come to regard the process of connecting to my authentic self as "finding true north," this is my shorthand for finding one's true self underneath the self we are persuaded to become through social conditioning and the indoctrination into unhealthy perspectives.

Exploring what true north is (scientifically speaking) highlights how I view the relation:

> What is true north? True north is the direction that points directly towards the geographic North Pole. This is a fixed point on the Earth's globe.
>
> What is magnetic north—and why is it different to true north?
>
> True north is a fixed point on the globe. Magnetic north is quite different. Magnetic north is the direction that a compass needle points to as it aligns with the Earth's magnetic field.

Interestingly, the magnetic North Pole shifts and changes over time in response to changes in the Earth's magnetic core. It is not a fixed point.[1]

Loosely speaking, I view the "true north" as the fixed point within me—what I term, the "authentic self." Whereas "magnetic north" is the self we are encouraged to be by society—the person we may feel ourselves drawn to become in order to conform and gain validation in society.

When I make choices each day—both small and significant—I act on either my "true north" or my "magnetic north" —from either my fixed, ancient self or from the unfixed social identity I am compelled to pursue.

In real examples, it is the difference between "magnetically" adhering to the social identity, which defines achievement when you are in your formative years, or taking the time to determine your "true north" —your actual thoughts and emotions (as opposed to using those imprinted and projected onto you).

It is the difference between being a straight, feminine, married mother or being a queer, gender-nonconforming lesbian[2] who doesn't have children and who isn't married. It is the difference between being salaried, with the 401k, medical insurance, a house in suburbia or, by contrast, being a financially precarious poet, one-man-band business owner, who carries all her belongings in her car like a turtle.

In my experience, the difference between finding true north or heeding magnetic north is the difference between being emotionally and mentally authentic (health) or struggling with the side-effects of betraying the "true north" self to conform (albeit maladaptively) to the unfixed "magnetic north" self. Those side-effects and symptoms of this misalignment of life and identity can (among other ways) manifest as "mental illnesses" such as major Depressive Disorder, Dissociative Disorder, Generalized Anxiety Disorder, Complex Post Traumatic Stress Disorder, emotional flooding, depression with psychotic symptoms, suicidal ideation, self-harm, addiction, and ultimately a suicide attempt in the light of long-term mental and emotional abuse.

... The litany above is my actual "diagnosis." What does this speak to? My own failure, or weakness, or insanity? *No.* It speaks to the inwardly-violent nature of our attempts to become well-adjusted to situations that are, by their very nature, damaging and insane. It shows that most "mental illness" is, in fact, a sane reaction to an insane situation.

If the vast majority of the population is sick (ie: mental illness and/or physical illness), it tends to reason that the way of life (the structure that society has instituted on its people) is inherently unhealthy.

As a result of being propagated into a toxic way of life, the act of breaking from that life has been a rite of passage taken by those who wish to listen deep for their authentic self.

As a final thought . . . an interesting thing happens every few hundred years: magnetic North Pole and true north align. It is akin to a moment of eclipse wherein the life you have built intersects with the authentic/fixed self—and in the crossing, there is a reckoning as well as a recognizing—as we see what difference there is between what we have been made to be and who we truly are. This "aligning of norths" is also called mid-life; where these poems begin. They are echoes from the time of breakdown and breakthrough—scribbled in the gap between the lightning and the thunder as I counted the seconds . . . .

Leslie M. Browning

Northampton, Massachusetts
November 2021

THE PHOTOGRAPHY

*"When words become unclear, I shall focus with photographs.
When images become inadequate, I shall be content with silence."*
−ANSEL ADAMS

There are three threads to the story: the poems, the photographs, and the location pins. In following those, you follow the full story in all its enigmatic nature.

The poems within the collection do not tell the story of the place; the poems tell the story of me within the place. The poems speak to where I am at in my own life while traveling the landscape across the landscape in search of awe—the elusive substance that has the volume and mass to balance out even the heaviest of trauma.

The decision to include the photos is my effort to show reverence to that part of every story that cannot be put into words.

15   15

⊙ KINGS CANYON NATIONAL PARK, CALIFORNIA

A LAND ACKNOWLEDGMENT

Throughout this work, I cite locations along my travels. I used the well-known contemporary names for these places for ease of communal reference; however, the names of the land as quoted within this book have gone by many names in the languages of both the native peoples for whom they were home and eventually the European colonists who took these lands by force and duplicity. I honor this history and hold it within my mind/heart as I midwife my creative endeavors. While having these common language titles for places is referentially helpful for us as a global village, let us also remember that the land exists as a sentient being beyond labels, borders, and quantification.

"When we don't listen to our intuition, we abandon our souls. And we abandon our souls because we are afraid if we don't, others will abandon us."

—TERRY TEMPEST WILLIAMS

PART 1

THE TAMING

NOTES FROM THE LIFE
YOU ARE SOCIALIZED TO WANT

KODAK PROTRA 400   42

▶ 12   12

THE DISTANCE BETWEEN
HERE AND THERE

⊙ TRAIN FROM BOSTON, MASS. > WESTERLY, RHODE ISLAND

Pounding the chest

of the stillborn dreams,

the bodies are left

along the roadside.

The album of the never-had family

flashes across the flat glass of the train window

as it winds its way North across the night

    carrying me back

to the home that is no longer a home

to a life that is no longer your life,

and to a silence that is no longer empty.

THE WHOLE OF LIFE IN A DAY

◊ NAPATREE POINT, WATCH HILL, RHODE ISLAND

I have become, Mrs. Dalloway,

throwing parties to cover the silence.

Come with me to the lighthouse.

It is time to settle the unspoken.

I'll buy the flowers myself.

Scattering the pedals along the shore

so I can find my way back from the river.

THE RECKONING BEGINS

⊘ WHITE HORSE TAVERN, NEW YORK, NY

The drops of rain
   heavy
against the metal roof
   —frail.

The lights of traffic
   blurred
across the windsheild
   —streaked.

The stream of blood
   electric
down the windows
   —coursing.

The memories of lovers
   lost
cycling in my veins
   —poisoning.

The night road
   there
a dead reckoning
   —inescapable.

SEEKING SAVIORS
IN ALL THE WRONG PLACES

⊘ NEW HAVEN, CONNECTICUT

The

  bar

  at

  rock

  bottom,

and

  you

  had

  to

  walk

  through

  the

  door.

THE NEXT MORNING

⊙ NEW HAVEN, CONNECTICUT

Waning morning light
glowed behind the opaque, frosted
windows of the kitchen door.

Fierce sun cutting through
the starburst pattern cut into the glass
illuminated your brown eyes.

The heavy cream
cut and swirled
in the dark coffee.

Setting the plates in front of us,
I settled happily
into a new life.

KODAK PROTRA 400
42
►01

CYCLICAL WOUNDING

⟨ COLORADO SPRINGS, COLORADO

Adrift in the endless night,

I've wished on the stars far-flung

not knowing each spec of light

was the dust of my own dreams

shattered in another life

 —embedded in the horizon

 in the blast wave that shattered me

  into the mosaic of a

   melancholic,

  alcoholic

  dreamer

  drunk

on this insatiable yearning

to connect with another

because I can't find myself.

THE ROAD FROM SANTA FE
TO CIMARRON

⚲ TAOS, NEW MEXICO

Red dust,

sanguine from Sangre

bleeding into the snowy roads

that lead to the hidden mountain

where the lone buffalo waits.

KODAK PROTRA 400

42

12

12

VALENTINE

Which way is North?

Since you, I don't know up from down.

My trust in this compass

shattered in the *bosque* along the Rio

where everything would begin

and everything would end

with a snap of the saddle

      —you, bucked off—

        hitting the dusty ground,

      your disguise coming off in the chaos.

THE RECURRING DREAM

⦿ SANDIA MOUNTAIN, NEW MEXICO

In a land beyond the pervading dark,

in a state beyond the fever-pitch,

in a dialog beyond the finding of blame,

I'm hoping to find you

and build a home where we can

live the life we deserve.

KODAK PROTRA 400

Lobo

◊ White Sands National Park, New Mexico

Drive through the night
lost in the miles
a lone wayfarer
ever in motion.

Be gentle, Long Night
I don't belong here.
Thrown to the wolves,
I shifted nocturnal.

Arced up,
surrendered to
the glowing drum
of the full moon,
hear my cry.

WANDERLUST & OTHER DESERT TOWNS

⦿ TWENTYNINE PALMS HIGHWAY, JOSHUA TREE, CALIFORNIA

In that vintage shop,
outside of Joshua Tree,
where I picked up that ring
that spurred you to run
so I bought instead
that first faded bandanna ...

In the shamanic shifting sands,
in the middle of the golden hour,
at the heart of God's Country
we are present—without a past ...

In that spiraling Milky Way mesa
under the inky sky
at the center of the circling coyote's cry—
    part of me was left there
    to wander, wondering
    what might have been.

DIEZ

⟡ JOSHUA TREE, CALIFORNIA

Souls age in thousand-fold nights, wandering
across internal landscapes to desert's
edge. At the corner of a crossroad, a
blue tail flicks and slicks as the lizard
slides through dust, around adobe wall, and
disappears in the cracked door, cadmium
yellow deep. Landscapes converge, coyotes
howl, and the rattlesnake shakes, recoiling.
Milky way rivers run above sandy
scape. Daylight drown, watching stars emerge to
each the cure that lies in the slow silence.
I had a vision there—in the land of
thick heat and shifting sheer shapes. Rocks
stacked higgledy-piggledy by tired Gods
long-evaporated under midday
sun. They walked off down trails erased by winds
that keep secrets from time and memory.
It was there star-crossed and awe-struck my path
joined with a dark-eyed Delila seeking
my soul and the doorway into my world.
Trickster, temptress, bride, I can only hope as
I abide by the heart's pulling, following
her through trees, unto silhouetted horizon.

beneath the shadow
pound s a tiny HEART
chant ing for blue sky

DEEP CUTS, MINOR CHORDS

⊘ NEW HAVEN, CONNECTICUT

Muggy summer nights
leaving the kitchen door open
    inviting the soupy sea air
    steeping in the garden
to flow through the crumbling Victorian.

Among My Swan
echoing in electric waves
along those same pine floors
and up through the high ceilings.

The dirge sifting through the cracks
of plaster walls, slowly falling down.

… the ghosts of us still live there.
Long past everything else
being dead and gone.

A COWARD IN THE NIGHT,
DEATH, AND REBIRTH

⌖ CIMARRON, NEW MEXICO > YALE UNIVERSITY, NEW HAVEN, CONN.

A dark-haired specter of ill fate

emerged while back turned, taking

   the children I was to have,

   the life I was to lead,

   the person I was known to be.

Shot full of holes,

I pulled myself through heavy dirt

you piled on me.

You ended one life,

but I got another in me.

GUTSHOT

◊ EN ROUTE FROM AUSTIN, TEXAS >
THE COURTHOUSE, NEW HAVEN, CONNECTICUT

The lingering, languid lament

of what will inevitably come

to its conclusion, though can't

be quick and clean.

It's the bloody drawn-out scene

created by two cowards

who shot from the heart

rather than the hip.

Let me make this quick and painless.

I'll finish what you started.

*"Authenticity is a collection of choices that we have to make every day.
It's about the choice to show up and be real. The choice to be honest.
The choice to let our true selves be seen."*
— BRENE BROWN

PART 2

THE BREAKING

NOTES FROM THE ASYLUM

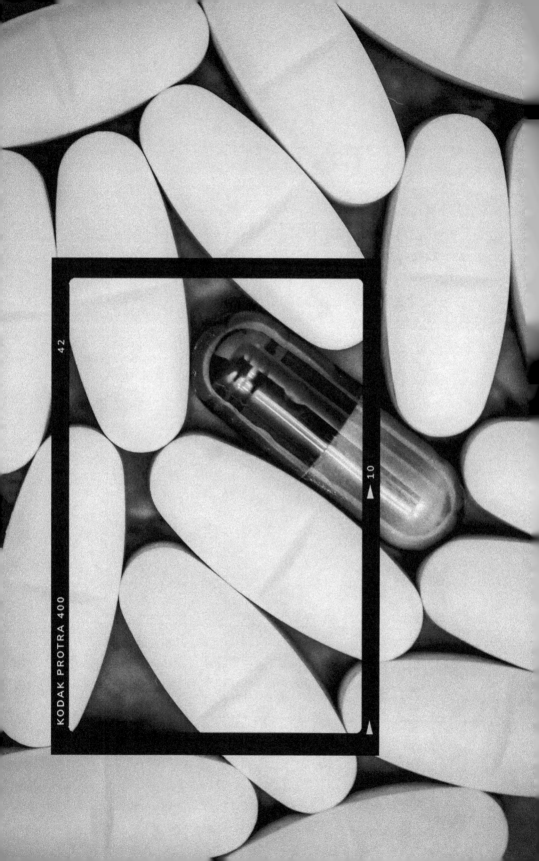

LIMBO

⊙ NEW HAVEN, CONNECTICUT

Beset in-between

a bereaved past

and a looming future

there is no present

only the anxiety

of all that has

   and will

    be lost.

E.M.D.R.

You summoned every hungry ghost
you roused every ravenous monster
you woke every ugly beast.
Then left me defenseless.

—I'm sorry, our time is up.

FOR WANT OF CARE

⊙ YALE PSYCH. INTENSIVE OUTPATIENT, NEW HAVEN, CONN.

In our youth
we have many a thing
with which to counter
the heaviness of living.

Passion, energy,
truth, resiliency,
ideals . . . hope for betterment.

Spent. Lost. Taken.
our unbalanced self
copes poorly, utilizing any
thing or substance that
dulls the harsh edges.

NERVE–SHAKEN

⊙ YALE PSYCH. CBT INTENSIVE OUTPATIENT, NEW HAVEN, CONN.

–for Shelly

What are we to do,
we who require silence
in a world of deafening din?

The far-flung corners being as far as they are,
where shall we carry ourselves?

Loud minds require
a quiet place, quite removed
from the happening and hazards.

Weary bones and frayed fibers
all are made whole
by steeping in a well-guarded calm.

WHITE SQUALL 41° NORTH

⦿ YALE PSYCH. CBT INTENSIVE OUTPATIENT, NEW HAVEN, CONN.

Heavy, heaving, hauling, mauling—

shifting, swift, sudden, swell—

torrent, turbulent, tossing, tempest—

dark, deep, drowning, deluge—

flowing, fitful, fleeting, flood—

of uncharted depth

and traumatic origin

swayed by the gravity of the mind.

This is the water I am swimming in.

GO ASK, ALICE

⦿ YALE PSYCH. DBT INTENSIVE OUTPATIENT, NEW HAVEN, CONN.

The thing they   don't   tell you

about being   over-medicated

is   that   you are   in fact ... over-medicated.

You are   just   left—

with a   deepened   sense of brokenness

  as you   shuffle along   like an Alzheimer's patient

who   cannot...   remember   what

they are...being treated   for—

exchanging one   insanity for   another.

Don't   believe me?

Go   ask, my   roommate.

I think   she'll know.

FINALLY TALKING WITH HIM ABOUT THE TWINS

⌖ WESTERLY, RHODE ISLAND
–for A.

It took a long time to use pronouns.
In obscurity, there was a safe distance.

You sprung it on me that morning
them instead of *it* without warning.

And for one last moment, there was an *us*
right before the end of you and I.

The last golden days
played out fast—a monochrome blur—
with flashes of red and deepest blue.

I forget where we were
before the empty cradle
came so harshly between us.

Let us remember the *before*
not the *during*
or the *after*.

So far down this road paved with good intentions
there is no other way but forward.

CLIFF—JUMPER

If I knew a way,

I would disconnect it

    —that part prone to needing.

Love is a binding

    —a blinding;

    —the one madness

        absent from the D.S.M.

I do all things with all that I am.

In this I will be made and destroyed

but in-between the leap and fall

I will live a legend, immortal.

UNADDRESSABLE

*"Our hospital was famous and housed many great poets and singers.
Did the hospital specialize in poets and singers or was it that poets
and singers specialized in madness?"* [4]

−SUSANNA KAYSEN, *GIRL, INTERRUPTED*

We did it, darling

—went all the way

   right

   off

   the

   edge

   in
             winning

   a
             the argument

   death
          at

   match
          all costs

   forsaking
        last word

   being *effective*
     had

   for being
     in

   right
       the

       suicide note

       I wrote

       but

       couldn't

       send.

THE RUNAWAYS

⊙ EN ROUTE FROM NEW HAVEN > WESTCHESTER, NEW YORK

I gave up my place of belonging

to lay down next to you

in the dark void

between all or nothing.

I can't get back the years

but maybe I will get back myself

... one day,

    some way

    no longer be a runaway.

CONSTELLATIONS OF WOUNDS

⊙ WESTCHESTER, NEW YORK

The patterns of the trauma align
across the memories of our mind
—inescapable—a blackhole of being.

8,947 miles later, I know now why
you refuse the say the names of those
        dead-to-you-yet-still-breathing
    —afraid as you are of the monsters
                    are still under the bed—
yet in the silence, you give them immortality.

Your ghastly ghosts
    —so cannibalistic in kind—
ate me alive while the little girl in you
daydreamed above the screams
of a life where
    I was wrong
        and you were right.

Years later,
I have become
one of the names you can't say
—I, the one who pulled back the sheets.

TOXIC AMNESIA

You see,

I forget.

I get lost

in what we *could have been*

and my boots

start back down

the path to you.

You see,

that is why.

I burned the bridge

so when I forget

where that path leads

there will be no going back.

THE LAWS OF GRAVITY

⟨ WESTCHESTER, NEW YORK

Expectations are sheer cliffs

we cannot help but climb.

The perfect, plumb ground too easy and expected

bears no liking for those beings without wings

but for whom heights hold draw.

Hope is a thing with feathers [5]

but does it know how to fly?

THINKING ABOUT IT ALL

about being homeless at age 8, when she left him (the first time)
and attending five different schools that year as we bounced from
refuge to refuge;

about when he almost killed her (the first time);

about the echoing question that followed me through my
childhood, "Is *it* a boy or a girl?" The perfect strangers asked
while staring.

about the addict-neighbors beating their children—screams
echoing daily through the thin walls of federal housing;

about the toddlers in the old neighborhood sitting out
in the parking lot with a straw snorting sand—
(because first we *see*, then we *learn*, then we *do*);

about the irony and fury of the teachers calling me *stupid* in class
because I couldn't read (because they couldn't teach);

about the table-turn circumstances of being accepted to college,
to picking through trash bins for cans so we could have milk and
bread, (because freedom from abusers comes at a cost);

about walking 5 miles to work every morning at 4:35 am in rain,
snow to make minimum wage from a man who banishes any
worker who dares whisper the word: *union;*

about seeing my leg for the first time with the splint off
—left ankle at a right angle—the black lightning running ink
deep—bolting up the break-lines in the bone . . . about the two
years it took to learn how to walk again;

about the dead-beat-dad, anthropomorphic, Abrahamic God
who was supposed to come but never did—(just like every other
father figure);

about the family that never was,
reflecting back at me in a bloody pool on the bathroom floor;

about this longing inside of me to have companionship and have
a husband and a family, but the confusing reality of being at odds
with men . . . and with myself;

about the grief-stricken look on his face when I told him I slept
with her—I am gay—and this life we've built together
is coming down.

about the echoing phrases of every xenophobic, homophobic slur I
overheard in conversation from ignorant blood-relations as a child
that silently invalidated;

about the revelation of finding her and by extension finding me,
only to learn what happens when you put a narcissists
on a pedestal (and then learn it again, because you go with
what you know);

    about the . . . about the . . . about the . . .
    all of it looping in relentless, reeling repetition.

HANGING IN BARDO

⊘ ELSEWHERE

In the vacuum of grief
the air was sucked from the room
    —past, present, future floated suspended—
        weightless.

In a fleeting moment of fierce clarity
    the bruised night sky
        —pulsed
then grew distant.

I left this place
and returned
to the dark womb.

In the exquisitely bleak
    fall.
In the suffocatingly abrupt
    arrival.

In the moments just before and
                . . . just after
tying the noose from the rope
you so meticulously wove for me.

WAKING UP ALIVE

⊘ SEMI-CONSCIOUS

The suspended weight
dropped—

The screaming lungs
broke—

The days dashed
reformed—

The drown stars
resurfaced—

The trembling screams
reverberated—

The numb legs
crumpled—

And there I was
gasping—

On the same carpet
facedown—

I clung to as a child
cowering—

WOUNDMATES

⊙ WESTCHESTER, NEW YORK

If we kept moving

   —blind in the blur

   of mileage mounting—

we might outrun the sun

and not see the sight awaiting

in the bare daylight

that we were the source

of each other's psychosis

and to *lose the madness*

would require roads

opposite in all ways.

ECLIPSE

⊙ WESTCHESTER, NEW YORK

You were at once
was my temple and my false god.

I would have
done anything *for* you.
—and you would have
done anything *to* me.

And in the coming
and the going
—therein
lies the danger.

NO BOUNDARIES

There was an eclipse
—sun and moon seeking saviors—
where two beings blurred into one.
               I, *the moon.*
       You, *the sun.*
Not knowing
               where you ended
       and I began,
the codependency of our cohabitation
brought about consequences of no coincidence.
As we converged, I at once found myself and
saw myself obliteration in the ascendancy of you.
Madness ensued in the eclipse
and as you began to pull from me,
I forgot that I was once solitary
I forgot, I am so much more
when not torn apart for the taking.

JUST GET IN THE DAMN CAR

⊘ ANYWHERE BUT HERE

You goaded me and grated me

laid out the revolver, stepped back,

blew out the light of the world

and invited the demon to dance

in the pale moonlight, beside that

pond where you sang for me

and helped me set my heartbeat to

a song that calls you back to

a country life, reminding you of

the waiting car leading, as ever,

on the road.

"Thousands of tired, nerve-shaken, over-civilized people are beginning to find out that going to the mountains is going home; that wildness is a necessity"
    –JOHN MUIR"

PART 3

THE BOLTING

FINDING THE FERAL SELF

Roman Candle in the Night

📍Kings Canyon, California

Shame be damned—own the ruin of yourself.
Wear the failure like a vintage coat
    —torn, tattered heart—
        you are a worn-out classic,
a soul of arcane salt and grit.

Outcast,
    iconoclast,
            stand fast.
Beyond the black and white blah of button-down norm
                we clash and crash
        in the candle-lit dusk
of conscious dreams and darkest desires

I return to the wild,
dig my heels in,
bare my teeth,
and stand this new ground.

RISE

You didn't dig the hole deep enough
the bleached skeletons surfaced at each rain

You didn't dig the hole deep enough
the toxic waste seeped into the groundwater.

You didn't dig the hole deep enough
to come out the other side of her lies.

You didn't dig the hole deep enough
to swallow all of me, some part remembered.

You didn't dig the hole deep enough.
… that was the only reason I survived.

SIRENS

⟨ DEAD HORSE POINT, MOAB, UTAH

Driving off the cliff

is much less glamorous than depicted

in the flicks where the camera cuts

before the bloody landing

and bone-cracking burns

as the very fuel that freed you

        consumes you.

KODAK PR

42

16

FREEDOM

♀ CANYON LANDS, MOAB, UTAH

Thank you for shattering
the window of white picket dreams
I'd grown tired of imagining
an equally-unattainable union
of compromised identities
and negotiated silences.

Beyond the Wonderwall
of what could have been,
there is the wild, fierce awe
of what is ahead of us
on the long passage
through the night of denial.

64

HUNGRY GHOSTS

♀ LEAVING LAS VEGAS

Red lights mix with rain
        —spilling blood
    across the windshield.

Not a road long enough
to outrun the dawn.

The darkness hums
with deafening regret.

Walking the wet streets,
seeking absolution.

Finding only
the ghost of us.

Not a road long enough
to outrun the dawn.

Let the sun rise.
I am ready.

GOING TO SEE THE SHAMAN

⊘ BRYCE CANYON, UTAH

–for Frank

Tracing the hummingbird
around the Navajo Loop,
noose marks 'round my neck,
how, brother, do I move past
all that has happened?

The only thing I have ever seen to work
    was, despite trauma, to become
a wholesome power generated from within,
that is cultivated and expanded
    to the point that
all previous attempts by other
at obliteration are rendered irrelevant
because they simply don't compare
    in terms of
power, vibration, frequency, or influence.

WITHOUT DESTINATION

Don't look for a glint of the divine.
Enjoy the light as the sun arcs in season.
Breath in the dust, and ground yourself.
Get dirt under the fingernails—live a life—
with the blood and mud,

      shame and need

      regret and blame.

There will be a time for
lying lazy, along the unfolded summer night.
Now is the time of the fleeting,

      the fierce,

      the sunlit days

      and rolling nights.

When we just ride
through the night and 'round again
—*third star to the right and straight on*

      to the morning.

IN SANTA FE WITH TIM LEARY

⚲ SOMEWHERE IN BETWEEN IT ALL

–for Joanna

Bobby, I followed the blood on the tracks
and found her walking them barefoot
     —guitar strapped to her back—
leading me back to the night we met.

The gutted night of Technicolor dreams
eyes shattered like glittering ice
stars scattered in the vast night.

A desert hare, neither here nor there,
heralds the pendulous horizon swing,
pulling the moon into day and sun into night.

Lost in the eclipse
I resurface in the dawning moonlight to tribal echoes
     pulling me through bardo
to push on down the abandoned routes
where the red-tails wait like signposts
guiding me home to the high-desert mountains.

SAVE YOURSELF

◊ TUSCON, ARIZONA

Belonging to no one,

I belong to everyone

having no home,

I belong where my boots rest.

Accepting no keeper

I can pull up stakes

ride unto the new horizon

post-up in the field of bison

dancing with the dust devil

tumbleweed a crown of thorns

I will die for my own sins

and rise three days later,

my own savior.

KODAK PROTRA 400   42

16

THE DIRGE

⦾ GEMINI BRIDGES, MOAB, UTAH

Roaming across the land
of dazzling desolation
I seize freedom by unearthing
the beauty in the vanishing
nature of all that is vital.

Knowing that I will survive
the death of all I hold dear,
and howl upon the alter
as the pyre burns,
the soul churns,
and the body yearns
for what is now ash.

THE TECHNICOLOR BURNING BUSH

⦿ TEXARKANA, TEXAS

In the misty morning

beyond murky mirages

I hear the voice of God in the hum

of the neon sign at the rest stop

where the caravan of displaced desperadoes

and expats post-up for the

bottomless cup of coffee

at the nighthawk counter

where Mary is selling her life for a dollar a table.

She calls my prodigal-self, Hun

and for the whole of the blue plate special

I am not an orphan.

A Sparkle of Knowing
◎ Canyonlands, Moab, Utah

The inane, the tame
this insanity of inert stability
well-manicured lies of contentment
and normalcy, white washing the wildness
engrained in the lineage of this liberated
stray who isn't built for the unsettled
but is too feral for formality.

Burn it down, dear one
—burn it all down.

KODAK PROTRA 400   42   KODAK PROTRA 400   42

► 01

DESERT DESCENT

♀ THE DELICATE ARCH TRAIL, MOAB, UTAH

Black hat's brim
tipped down against the sun
drenched to the bone
the road is home.

The open field aching
the scar-tissue wrapped soul
settles stiff and achy
when not in motion.

The golden hour
blue mesa silhouetted
on a wild-fire horizon
    —burning amber
     in a deepening dark.

The juniper trembles.
Night falls.

83

UNSPOKEN

⌖ PETRIFIED FOREST, ARIZONA

There are things that will go unsaid
and unwritten—that will live in us alone
until time shifts the landscape of memory
and all that we remember is changed.

Out beyond the murkiness left
by anger-tinted arguments,
remember what you know in your heart
and bring that truth close.

For a moment let it be.
For a moment love it as-is.
For a moment hold it
then leave it along the roadside.

WILDFIRE

◊ BIG SUR, CALIFORNIA

Go West, young woman.
Drive through the night.

You're not abandoned
    you're liberated.
You're not crazy
    you're human.
They're not right,
    they're repressed.

Gaslit, gagged, uprooted, inverted
reclaim what you lost
in the cage of the white picket fence.

Go West, young woman
—*drive through the night.*

Tear up the road behind you.
There is no way back.

ADVICE FROM A STRAY

⟨ SAN FRANCISCO, CALIFORNIA

Bridled, broken, muzzled

stop trusting these upright animals

rejoin the pack—plant your feet—

belly up, *howl.*

MUSTANG

⌖ WEST HOLLYWOOD, CALIFORNIA

–for R.

Ride this life hard

—barebacked, bone-shaken.

Wrap your legs tight

—thighs around her rib cage, pounding.

Take hold in the rush

—fingers tangled in her mane, entwined.

Look up at me—meet my eyes—stay here with me,

there is nothing back there for you.

COUNTING COUP

⊘ JUST PASSING THRU

You weren't the first
you won't be the last.

Across this starry night
I drive, with nothing to my name
but the intangible album
of connections forged and waned.

These are not incidences of madness
but seasons of alchemy—
turning from lies to truth.

You were the latest lesson.
    You broke me,
    but I am still wild.

JUST LET IT BE

◊ SEDONA, ARIZONA

Swing high into the stars
look down into the desert—

Let yourself break.
That's when the truth spills out
—with the blood and tears
that precedes all birth.

Swing high into the stars
look down into the desert's
                desolation dazzling
the solitude is a stripping away
of the muscle holding bone

Swing high into the stars.
Let responsibility go to ruin
the wild winds are calling
       —carrying the whispers
         of the ancestors
who have never left you.

THE LAST EXIT

The pulse of the highway beats
as the white stripes tick by
—slip under the car
and into the rearview.

Clouds settle low
on the horizon
—like windswept watercolor
in muted mesa blues.

I roam the rolling road
a caravan of red light pilgrims
—blurred, white-hot wanderlust
weaving into a cobalt sky.

We've gaslit the gods.
At all-night truck stops, they shuffle along
—afraid they've damned us all
when it was we who damned them.

Through the haze of an indigo,
indica dream, the signs rise
—hobo hieroglyphics tell tale
that this is a safe place. *Is it true?*

KODAK PROTRA 400   42   KODAK PROTRA 400   42

►01   ►

►01   ►   ►

KODAK PROTRA 400

NEON TRAILS & THE WILD UNKNOWN

⦿ TUCUMCARI, NEW MEXICO

There are times
when all I can take in
lies between my headlights.

Roaming the road,
I am not alone.
I contain multitudes.

At least,
that's what the good book says—
    the vagabond's bible
    on the nightstand.

Posting up in the fallout motel along Route 66
praying to the patron saint of perpetual motion
—have mercy on us—we who are going and going,
                    never arriving.

There is only so far
this old car can bring me.

We drive through the night
only to crawl out of the car
on all-fours.

The end of the road
is the beginning
of *the wild unknown.*

*"I knew that the real was yonder
and that the darkened dream of it was here."*

—BLACK ELK

PART 4

THE RECLAIMING

NOTES FROM BECOMING WILD

THIS IS WHAT YOU SHALL DO *AND NOT DO*

Know your worth, know your limits, know your boundlessness, know your strengths, know your weaknesses, know your accomplishments, and know your dreams.

Be a mirror for all those who project their darkness onto you; do not internalize it. Don't seek validation from those who will refuse to understand you. Don't say *yes,* when you need to say *no.* Don't stay when you know you should go. Don't go when you know you should stay. Respond, don't react. Behave in a manner aligning with your values.

Sleep. Seek out quiet. Don't glorify busyness. Reignite your curiosity for the world. Explore new horizons. Be honest with yourself. Be gentle with yourself. Approach yourself as you would approach a child—with a kind tone and deep understanding. Love yourself or, at the very least, have mercy on yourself. Be your own parent, your own child, your own lover, your own partner.

Give less of your time to employment that drains you of your enthusiasm for life. Reclaim your freedom by redefining your necessities. Take that gathered energy; devote your precious life to your passions.

Unplug from the babble. Seek awe. It is the counterbalance to trauma. Do your psychological work, and don't take any one else's work upon yourself. Protect your peace. Listen to what your heart knows; *fuck* everything else.

CATALOGING THE CROSSING

⦿ WAYFARER FARM, BERKSHIRE MOUNTAINS, MASS

Losing them.

Leaving him.

Leaving her.

Finding her.

Reckoning her.

Becoming me.

Reckoning me.

Reckoning us.

Claiming queer.

Reconciling all.

Gutting him.

Wanting her.

Dying

Following her.

Trying

Embracing me.

Lying.

Fighting.

Running.

Protecting her.

Agreeing.

Loving her.

Seeing.

Obeying her.

Fleeing.

Hating her.

Needing her.

Riding.

Hoping.

Unmasking her.

Writing.

Seeing her.

Making.

Losing me.

Offering.

Losing it.

Visiting.

Leave it.

Listening.

Answering.

Admitting.

Beginning.

DIALOGUES ALONG THE STREAM OF CONSCIOUSNESS

⚲ WAYFARER FARM, BERKSHIRE MOUNTAINS, MASS

The shell-shocked protector who comes out when I'm triggered
has their now-maladaptive roots in attempting to manage
the unmanageable. Thirty-five years later, I can still remember the
nights I spent curled up with the dog in the corner of my child-
hood room—rooted fearfully into the thick carpet—as I listened
to him beat her in his strung-out madness. …that part was born
the night the eight-year-old picked up a bat and kicked in the door.

Call that part of me "broken," call it "mean," call it "madness,"
call it a "psychiatric disorder;" it was what part of me needed to
become to survive the war waged.

I've heard many overlapping stories from those who have survived
their own suicide attempt. So many of us look back on the
escalation to action, and recall that moment—of fierce,
crystalline clarity. As terrible and beautiful as it was, we awe at it,
all the while knowing if we ever experience it again,
it will be too late.

RITES & THE ALCHEMY OF RESURRECTION

WAYFARER FARM, BERKSHIRE MOUNTAINS, MASS

Power is truth beyond manipulation.
In the turning of the great wheel,
the reckoning comes for us all.

Hanging my hat
taking off my boots
watching the hawk spiral in the dawning light,
I now watch the storm come for you.

All these years,
I thought I had to rebuild these bones
before I could be rid of you
when all I had to do was double down.

To steal my voice back from
fight, flight, and fawn,
and *own* my journey
with radical authenticity.

All along,
it wasn't me
who feared the dawn.
I am the dawn.

WHEN IT IS FIXIN' TO STORM

⊘ WAYFARER FARM, BERKSHIRE MOUNTAINS, MASS

Go now. Go West
—go toward yourself.

Take that freedom and ride it to the coast
—until it breaks down or builds up.

Wear those old boots again
—the ones that peeled apart at the sole

        only to be remade.

Let the grief burn
—let it hollow you out

Just let it be what it was
    —sit with it,
    hear it,
    feel it,
    follow it,
    then listen.

… drive through the night, darlin'.
The only way home,
is through.

SAYING GOODBYE

⊘ WAYFARER FARM, BERKSHIRE MOUNTAINS, MASS

–for Mallory

She will always remember
what she did . . .
and what was almost lost.

Hurt people;
  hurt
  people.

In denial there is dis-integration
—the pieces of the self war with each other—
  and there is collateral damage.

I only wish I could have one more talk
            with the young girl
    —the one before *him* . . .
    —the one I met that night beside the pond . . .
    —the reason I stayed so long.

FLASH FLOOD

⚲ WAYFARER FARM, BERKSHIRE MOUNTAINS, MASS

The dried up creek

still sees a flash flood now and again

the waters come rolling down the

the river of hell's high water

running through my mind.

I've learned to let the water flow

but not drown with you.

The waters come.

The waters go.

I remain.

UNCONDITIONAL LOVE

⚲ WAYFARER FARM, BERKSHIRE MOUNTAINS, MASS

–for M & T

I don't come back this way much
passing through—
these shadowlands
    of blind love.

Sitting beside you,
in that old bed,
stuffed with tired battles,
the dogs sleeping heavy at our feet.

The seasoned memories
harden the heart more
with each passing winter
    as what we *were*
      and *could have been*
are composted to nourish *what is*
               and *will be.*

In the migration
from bardo to born,
I still miss the dogs.

KINFOLK

⦿ WAYFARER FARM, BERKSHIRE MOUNTAINS, MASS

–for Mom

Only mama is left,

only she stayed.

She leaves me now

at the foot of the mountains

that when one day I lose her

I will not be an orphan child.

THE TWO TREES

♀ WAYFARER FARM, BERKSHIRE MOUNTAINS, MASS

–for Kate Elizabeth Browning & James Andrew Browning

If you walk straight back

    —through the new growth that survived

      the logging in the 70s—

to the thick stands of hemlock

rooting along the edges and ledges

you will find them—

    the two trees

tucked under a blanket

of interconnected mycelium

    —the clothes of heaven—

guarded by the fairies

who travel with all stolen children.

Walk between the trees

    —where there is the thin place—

through the fields of heavy grasses,

    until you reach the old stone house.

I'll be waiting for you.

THIS DIRT

⚲ WAYFARER FARM, BERKSHIRE MOUNTAINS, MASS

The minerals in these borrowed bones

soon to be returned

to the great womb

from which we all take root.

But not quite yet . . .

This soul isn't finished with this body,

not when there are 15 acres to tend

    with these hands,

    this heart,

    settled into these old boots.

KODAK PROTRA 400

▶12

▶01

TRUE NORTH

⟡ALONG THE JEREMY RIVER, COLCHESTER, CONN.

–for Sara

I am attracted to unquantifiable things.
I want to look up,
while walking my own emotional terrain
wherein I felt so isolated,
and learn that I am not alone.

I seek to be surprised,
    to align, to be pulled in
—like gravity—longing for a touch
only without the danger
of the black holes of the past.

Are you there?
I thought I felt you brush past me
while in-between dream and waking.
Are you the echo of light from a star long dead
    or are you True North?

MY PROMISE TO YOU

⦿ WAYFARER FARM, BERKSHIRE MOUNTAINS, MASS

There is reason
in the madness.

There is a rising
in the descent.

There is release
in the rejection.

There is company
in the isolation.

There is meaning
in the senseless.

There is strength
in the helplessness.

There is belonging
in the abandonment.

There is truth
in the deception.

There is fullness in the grief.
There is release in the surrender.

There is maturity
in the idealism.

There is momentum
in the turmoil.

There is value
in the waste.

There is rebirth
in the death.

There is freedom in the destruction.
...all you have to do is survive it.

CLOSING NOTE

At their core, I believe all creative endeavors embody the processing of emotion that cannot otherwise be expressed and regaining agency and power after being made to feel helpless by abusers, illnesses, death, poverty, violence.... More than any other work that came before it in my writing career, *Drive through the Night* speaks to this fact.

"Doing the work" and "finding closure"...these terms that drive us through our healing processes. But it wasn't until the last few years—during this alignment of true north and magnetic north that I call "mid-life," that I have understood these secondhand terms in an intimate, day-to-day sense.

For me, *closure* may as well be a four-letter word. I seek closure the way a man on fire seeks water. "I'm seeking closure." What does that statement even mean—in a realistic sense?

At its simplest, I've come to regard closure as the process of feeling the emotions that demand to be felt. It is giving yourself permission to have all the feelings you are actually having. It is the process of re-training yourself to feel your emotions without repressing them and, just as importantly, without judging them. You don't have to "solve" or "fix" the emotions being felt—just, let them be—find a place where you are safe to just let the emotions come. Feel the emotions to their full depth. Sit with them. Tolerate them. Feel as they intensify and soften within you as you process the full circle of the emotion itself.

"Doing the work" is a weighty undertaking I respect in others. "Doing the work" is shorthand for a commitment to knowing ourselves and being responsible for our emotional presence in this life. It is getting up every day and meeting myself where I am at (rather than projecting upon myself where I hoped I'd be in my healing). It is a commitment to feeling what demands to be felt. It is selecting which thoughts to engage from within the flowing consciousness and letting those thoughts that do not serve me continue on down the river.

"Doing the work" is the term for gathering the trauma within me and alchemizing it into something of use and purpose rather than simply allowing the hurt within me to leech out and hurt others.

All the abuse I endured resulted from another person not doing their own work and thereby projecting their unaddressed suffering out to others. It is where we get the adage, "hurt people, hurt people."

I have become an emotional tracker within the dense woods of my life's journey. I continue to acquire the skills to discern the root of the emotions from amongst the old-growth stands of trauma looping in my past shadow across the present path.

I have become a forager of connections—noticing the recurring/ familiar feelings and following the emotional mycelium interconnecting all the root experiences and intentions holding you to this existence.

Looking back over the book—over the years in my life it represents—I can (now) clearly see the parts of the journey.

The "taming" is the process of being taught (punishment-reward style) what emotions are and are not acceptable—you're being taught what you are allowed to feel and not allowed to feel. We are tamed by all manner of narcissists—societal, governmental, warmongering, religious, capitalist, parental, familial, spousal—

The "breaking" is when you start imposing those "rules" on yourself—limiting yourself as to what you will allow yourself to feel and what you will not. It is when the authentic self is metaphorically "broken" and trained to be and do what society requires of us.

The "reclaiming" is the powerful turning point wherein you feel all that has gone unfelt throughout your life and, in doing so, come to know yourself for the first time in your adult life. You are reclaiming yourself, and are valuing your right to feel and be who you authentically are. It is the process of normalizing options outside of the expected path. It starts very simply by allowing your authentic self to feel what you truly actually are feeling. And learning how not to judge the feelings or judge yourself for having them. Make space for them—contain that space if you must—but allow them to be . . . allow yourself to just be . . . without judgment. Acting on the feelings isn't always justified, but this doesn't mean the feelings are wrong or invalid. Feels are the response to experience—any response is valid.

Finally, "becoming wild" is the becoming of, not only our authentic self but, our feral self—the wild soul that we were born to be uninhibited by notions of social norms. The civilizing/socialization of this wild heart in order to better conform to what we are supposed to be, and want, and do" —the process of learning how to deny the instincts that are meant to inform my state of self and help me navigate my needs. We are taught what we should instead feel and do and want and pursue. To "become wild" is the process of leaving the cage and acclimating to instinct and agency.

In the end, *Drive through the Night,* is a commitment to doing the work until you reach the other side of what lies between your past and your future. I hope I always have it in me to push through the fatigue and cover that mileage . . . actively seeking awe along the way.

ENDNOTES

1 *True north and magnetic north: What's the difference?* Royal Museums Greenwich. (n.d.). Retrieved May 9, 2021, from https://www.rmg.co.uk/stories/topics/true-north-magnetic-north-whats-difference.

2 I use the terms for gender and sexual identity that we currently have, with full knowledge that future generations will continue to evolve these definitions further—or do away with them completely. I release these words in hoping that those future generations will see past the fixed language/terms to the heart of my meaning.

3 "White Rabbit" song written by Grace Slick and recorded by the American rock band Jefferson Airplane for their 1967 album *Surrealistic Pillow*

4 Kaysen, S. (1999). *Girl, interrupted*. Vintage Books.

5 Emily Dickinson, "'Hope' is the Thing with Feathers" from *The Complete Poems of Emily Dickinson*, edited by Thomas H. Johnson, ed., Cambridge, Mass.: The Belknap Press of Harvard University press, Copyright © 1951, 1955, 1979, 1983 by the President and Fellows of Harvard College. Reprinted by permissions of the publishers and Trustees of Amherst College.

6 Kerouac, J., &; Cunnell, H. (2008). *On the road: The original scroll*. Penguin Books.

7 Barrie, James, Matthew (2020). *Peter and Wendy or Peter Pan*. WiseHouse Classics.

8 Brown C. Brené. (2010). *The gifts of imperfection let go of who you think you're supposed to be and embrace who you are*.

9 Muir, J. (2001). *Our national parks*. Ross and Perry, Inc.

FOLLOW

digital basecamp : www.lmbrowning.com

facebook : @authorLMbrowning

instagram : @wildsilence_lmbrowning

instagram : @wayfarer_farm

photography : www.wildsilence.myportfolio.com

ABOUT THE AUTHOR

(L.M.) Leslie M. Browning is the award-winning author of twelve titles. She grew up in the small fishing village of Stonington, Connecticut. In her writing, Browning explores the confluence of the natural landscape and the interior landscape. She is a convergence of her flannel-clad New England roots and the wide-sky, high-desert of the Southwest.

Over the course of her career to date, Browning has garnered several awards, including: five Pushcart Prize nominations, two *Foreword Reviews'* Awards, and the Nautilus Gold Medal for Poetry.

In 2011, she founded Homebound Publications & Divisions, which has gone on to become a leading independent publisher in the country. She has served two terms on the Board of Directors for the Independent Book Publisher's Association, is a Fellow with the International League of Conservation Writers, and recently became a Tree Ambassador with One Tree Planted.

Following the release of her micro memoir, *To Lose the Madness*, in 2018 Leslie was invited to present at Yale University's TEDx Conference entitled, "Uncharted" to share her own journey with successive trauma and search for transcendence in her talk, *Writing on Life*.

Browning holds a degree in Philosophy from the University of London and a Liberal Bachelor or Arts focusing on English, Psychology, and Digital Media from Harvard University. She currently serves on both the State of Connecticut's Suicide Advisory Board and CT-NAMI's Attempt Survivor/Lived Experience Committee working remove the stigma of mental illness through storytelling and activism.

A vagabond-turned-homesteader, Les is currently posted-up in the Berkshire Mountains of Massachusetts where she is solo homesteading 15-acres of raw land, creating her own modern Walden.

HOMEBOUND
PUBLICATIONS

Since 2011 We are an award-winning independent publisher striving to ensure that the mainstream is not the only stream. More than a company, we are a community of writers and readers exploring the larger questions we face as a global village. It is our intention to preserve contemplative storytelling. We publish full-length introspective works of creative non-fiction, literary fiction, and poetry.

Look for Our Imprints Little Bound Books, Owl House Books,
The Wayfarer Magazine, Wayfarer Books & Navigator Graphics

WWW.HOMEBOUNDPUBLICATIONS.COM

WAYFARER

BASED IN THE BERKSHIRE MOUNTAINS, MASS.

The Wayfarer Magazine. Since 2012, *The Wayfarer* has been offering literature, interviews, and art with the intention to inspires our readers, enrich their lives, and highlight the power for agency and change-making that each individual holds. By our definition, a wayfarer is one whose inner-compass is ever-oriented to truth, wisdom, healing, and beauty in their own wandering. *The Wayfarer's* mission as a publication is to foster a community of contemplative voices and provide readers with resources and perspectives that support them in their own journey.

Wayfarer Books is our newest imprint! After nearly 10 years in print, *The Wayfarer Magazine* is branching out from our magazine to become a full-fledged publishing house offering full-length works of eco-literature!

Wayfarer Farm & Retreat is our latest endeavor, springing up the Berkshire Mountains of Massachusetts. Set to open to the public in 2024, the 15 acre retreat will offer workshops, farm-to-table dinners, off-grid retreat cabins, and artist residencies.

WWW.WAYFARERBOOKS.ORG

CPSIA information can be obtained
at www.ICGtesting.com
Printed in the USA
JSHW020602270222
R11466800001B/R114668PG23289JSX00001B/1

9 781953 340450